PRINCEWILL LAGANG

Authentic Communication: Speaking Your Truth in Love

This book was professionally typeset on Reedsy.
Find out more at reedsy.com

Contents

1

Introduction

Welcome to the journey of exploring the intricacies of authentic communication within relationships. In this book, we embark on a quest to understand the art of connecting deeply with those around us through honest and heartfelt expression. Communication is the lifeblood of any relationship, and its authenticity forms the foundation upon which trust, intimacy, and mutual understanding are built.

The Focus of this Book

In a world where communication has become increasingly digital and fast-paced, the nuances of genuine connection can sometimes be overshadowed. This book shines a spotlight on the value of authentic communication as an essential element in creating and nurturing meaningful relationships. We will delve into various aspects of communication, from verbal exchanges to nonverbal cues, exploring how they contribute to the depth and authenticity of our connections.

The Significance of Authentic Communication

Honest and heartfelt communication is the bridge that enables us to truly understand and be understood by our loved ones. It goes beyond the surface and allows us to share our thoughts, feelings, and vulnerabilities openly. Through authentic communication, we create an environment where both parties can express themselves without fear of judgment, fostering an atmosphere of empathy and acceptance.

When we communicate authentically, we lay the groundwork for genuine intimacy. By sharing our true selves, we invite others to do the same, forging a bond that transcends superficial interactions. Authentic communication is the cornerstone of trust; it assures others that our words and actions are aligned, reducing misunderstandings and conflicts that can arise from miscommunication.

Navigating the Journey Ahead

Throughout the pages of this book, we will journey together through the realms of effective communication. We will explore strategies for active listening, empathetic responses, and cultivating self-awareness. Additionally, we will delve into the challenges that may arise when striving for authenticity in communication and provide practical guidance on overcoming these obstacles.

Remember, the goal of this exploration is not perfection but progress. As we learn and apply the principles of authentic communication, we equip ourselves with the tools to foster deeper connections and more fulfilling relationships. So, let's embark on this adventure together, unraveling the threads of communication that bind us and discovering the art of true connection.

As we delve into each chapter, keep in mind that authentic communication is a skill that can be cultivated and refined over time. Through dedication and practice, we can transform our relationships and enrich our lives through the power of heartfelt expression.

2

The Power of Authentic Communication

In a world where superficial interactions have become commonplace, the power of authentic communication cannot be understated. This chapter delves into the profound impact that genuine and open communication can have on relationships, highlighting how authenticity serves as a catalyst for building trust, fostering understanding, and nurturing emotional intimacy.

Building Trust Through Authenticity

Authentic communication is the cornerstone of trust within relationships. When we communicate honestly and transparently, we demonstrate a level of integrity that reassures others of our intentions. This integrity forms the foundation of trust, allowing individuals to rely on our words and actions. Trust is the glue that binds relationships together, and authenticity is what solidifies that bond.

Fostering Understanding

At the heart of authentic communication lies the desire to be truly understood and to understand others in return. When we communicate openly, we invite others into our thoughts, emotions, and experiences. This transparency not only gives others insight into our perspectives but also encourages them to reciprocate. As we actively listen and engage with one another's authentic expressions, we bridge gaps in understanding and create a sense of unity.

Nurturing Emotional Intimacy

Emotional intimacy is the ability to share one's deepest feelings, desires, and fears with another person. Authentic communication paves the way for this intimacy by creating an environment where individuals feel safe to express themselves without fear of judgment. When we reveal our vulnerabilities and insecurities, we invite a reciprocal vulnerability from others. This mutual openness fosters a deeper emotional connection that goes beyond surface-level interactions.

Overcoming Barriers to Authentic Communication

While the benefits of authentic communication are clear, it's important to acknowledge the challenges that can arise. Society's norms, past experiences, and fear of vulnerability can all act as barriers to authentic expression. Overcoming these barriers requires a willingness to confront discomfort and engage in self-reflection. By acknowledging and addressing these obstacles, we can pave the way for more genuine and fulfilling connections.

The Practice of Authentic Communication

Authentic communication is not a passive endeavor; it requires practice and intentionality. It involves active listening, empathetic responses, and a commitment to being present in conversations. Practicing authenticity also means embracing imperfection. Mistakes may happen, misunderstandings may arise, but the foundation of authentic communication lies in the willingness to address these challenges openly and work through them together.

Conclusion

As we conclude this chapter, it's evident that authentic communication holds transformative power within relationships. Through genuine expression and a commitment to understanding, we can build trust, foster intimacy, and create lasting connections. The journey toward authentic communication requires courage, vulnerability, and a genuine desire to connect with others on a profound level. With each conversation and interaction, we have the opportunity to harness this power and shape the course of our relationships in meaningful ways.

3

Defining Authentic Communication

At the heart of every meaningful interaction lies the concept of authentic communication. This chapter delves into the depths of this essential practice, breaking down its components and exploring how it encompasses vulnerability, honesty, and active listening. By understanding what authentic communication truly entails, we equip ourselves with the tools to cultivate more genuine and fulfilling relationships.

Understanding Authentic Communication

Authentic communication goes beyond the exchange of words; it is a profound form of connection that involves conveying our true thoughts, feelings, and experiences to others. It is about being genuine and transparent in our interactions, allowing ourselves to be seen and heard as our authentic selves. This practice transcends societal masks and reveals the core of who we are.

Embracing Vulnerability

Central to authentic communication is the act of vulnerability. When we communicate authentically, we open ourselves up to the possibility of being hurt or misunderstood. By sharing our fears, insecurities, and hopes, we invite others to connect with us on a deeper level. Vulnerability is a bridge that spans the gap between individuals, fostering empathy and understanding.

Practicing Honesty

Honesty is a pillar of authentic communication. It involves speaking truthfully, not only about facts but also about our emotions and intentions. Honesty allows us to build trust with others, as they come to rely on our words and actions as genuine reflections of our thoughts and feelings. Authentic communication requires us to confront discomfort and have candid conversations even when they might be difficult.

The Art of Active Listening

Active listening is another essential facet of authentic communication. It's about being fully present and engaged when others speak, not just waiting for our turn to talk. Active listening involves not only hearing the words being spoken but also understanding the emotions and context behind them. By demonstrating that we value and respect what others have to say, we create a space for authentic communication to flourish.

Creating a Safe Space

To foster authentic communication, it's crucial to create a safe and nonjudgmental environment. When individuals feel secure expressing themselves without fear of criticism, they are more likely to open up and share their true thoughts and feelings. This safe space nurtures the growth of deeper connections and encourages ongoing authentic interactions.

Challenges and Growth

Authentic communication is not without its challenges. Overcoming the fear of judgment, navigating disagreements, and addressing misunderstandings can be difficult. However, each challenge presents an opportunity for growth. By acknowledging these obstacles and working through them with empathy and understanding, we strengthen the foundation of our relationships.

Conclusion

As we conclude this chapter, it's clear that authentic communication is a dynamic practice that requires intentionality and effort. It involves vulnerability, honesty, and active listening, all of which contribute to the depth and authenticity of our interactions. By embracing these components and continually refining our communication skills, we pave the way for more meaningful and genuine connections with those around us.

4

Breaking Down Barriers

I n the pursuit of authentic communication, we often encounter barriers that hinder our ability to connect deeply with others. This chapter dives into some common barriers, including the fear of judgment and other obstacles that impede genuine expression. By understanding these challenges and learning how to overcome them, we can pave the way for open and authentic communication.

Fear of Judgment: A Formidable Barrier

One of the most prevalent barriers to authentic communication is the fear of judgment. This fear stems from the worry that if we express our true thoughts, feelings, or vulnerabilities, we will be met with criticism, rejection, or misunderstanding. This fear can be deeply ingrained and can prevent us from fully engaging in honest and open conversations.

The Impact of Past Experiences

Past experiences also contribute to communication barriers. If we've encountered situations where our authenticity was met with negative reactions, we might become hesitant to share openly again. These past wounds can lead us to put up emotional walls, preventing us from engaging in conversations with the depth and vulnerability required for authentic communication.

Overcoming Barriers: Creating a Safe Space

To overcome barriers to authentic communication, it's essential to create a safe space for expression. Here are some strategies to break down these barriers and foster a nurturing environment:

1. Practice Empathy: Show empathy and understanding towards others' perspectives. When people feel heard and validated, they are more likely to reciprocate.

2. Lead by Example: Demonstrate vulnerability and authenticity yourself. By modeling open communication, you encourage others to do the same.

3. Active Listening: Engage in active listening, focusing on understanding the speaker's emotions and concerns. This promotes a sense of trust and mutual respect.

4. Nonjudgmental Attitude: Cultivate a nonjudgmental attitude in conversations. Assure others that their thoughts and feelings are valued, regardless of agreement.

5. Encourage Openness: Encourage others to express themselves freely without fear of repercussions. Reinforce that you are there to listen and understand, not to criticize.

6. Acknowledge Emotions: Recognize and validate emotions. Let others know that it's okay to feel the way they do, and create space for them to explore those emotions further.

Self-Reflection and Personal Growth

Overcoming communication barriers also requires introspection and personal growth. Take time to reflect on your own fears and insecurities that might be affecting your ability to communicate authentically. Seek to understand the root causes of these barriers and work towards addressing them.

Conclusion

In the journey toward authentic communication, it's important to acknowledge and address the barriers that stand in our way. Fear of judgment and past experiences can create emotional walls that hinder genuine expression. However, by actively working to create a safe space for open dialogue, practicing empathy, and encouraging vulnerability, we can break down these barriers and foster an environment where authentic communication can thrive. As we navigate these challenges, we strengthen our connections and create relationships that are built on understanding, trust, and true intimacy.

5

Speaking Your Truth

Chapter 5: Speaking Your Truth

At the core of authentic communication lies the ability to speak your truth – to express your thoughts, feelings, and needs honestly and openly. This chapter delves into the significance of authentic self-expression and provides insights into techniques that enable you to communicate your truth with respect, compassion, and clarity. By mastering the art of speaking your truth, you empower yourself to foster deeper connections and create a more genuine environment for communication.

The Importance of Honest Expression

Speaking your truth is a fundamental aspect of authentic communication. It involves conveying your thoughts and emotions openly, without pretense or suppression. When you express your true feelings and needs, you create an opportunity for genuine understanding and connection. Honest expression not only promotes mutual respect but also encourages others to reciprocate with their own authenticity.

Balancing Truth with Respect and Compassion

While speaking your truth is essential, it's equally important to do so with respect and compassion. Consider the impact your words may have on others and choose language that reflects your feelings without causing unnecessary harm. Honesty should be delivered in a way that fosters understanding rather than defensiveness or confrontation.

Techniques for Effective Expression

1. Use "I" Statements: Frame your statements using "I" to take ownership of your feelings. For example, say "I feel…" rather than "You make me feel…"

2. Practice Active Listening: Before expressing your truth, listen actively to the other person's perspective. This creates an environment of mutual respect and encourages them to listen to you in return.

3. Choose the Right Time and Place: Timing matters. Find a suitable moment when both parties are calm and receptive. Choose a private setting where you can have an uninterrupted conversation.

4. Avoid Blame and Judgment: Focus on your emotions and needs rather than assigning blame. This helps prevent defensiveness and promotes a solution-oriented discussion.

5. Be Specific: Clearly articulate your thoughts, emotions, and needs. Vague statements can lead to misunderstandings, while specifics provide clarity.

6. Seek Mutual Understanding: Invite the other person to share their perspective after you've expressed your truth. This demonstrates that you value their input and are open to a constructive dialogue.

7. Practice Patience: Authentic communication is a process. Be patient if the other person needs time to process your truth or respond.

Cultivating Emotional Intelligence

Emotional intelligence plays a pivotal role in speaking your truth effectively. Understanding your own emotions, recognizing those of others, and adapting your communication style accordingly contribute to more successful interactions. Emotional intelligence enables you to navigate conversations with sensitivity and empathy, promoting a deeper connection.

Conclusion

Speaking your truth is a powerful skill that contributes to the authenticity of your relationships. By expressing your thoughts, feelings, and needs honestly, you create a space for mutual understanding and connection. Through techniques like using "I" statements, practicing active listening, and balancing honesty with respect and compassion, you empower yourself to communicate effectively and nurture meaningful relationships. The art of speaking your truth not only enhances your own personal growth but also enriches the quality of your interactions, fostering an environment of trust, empathy, and true connection.

6

Active Listening and Empathy

In the realm of authentic communication, active listening and empathy shine as two essential pillars. This chapter explores the profound impact of these practices on building meaningful connections and fostering genuine understanding. By delving into the art of active listening and empathy, you equip yourself with invaluable tools that empower you to navigate conversations with depth and authenticity.

The Power of Active Listening

Active listening is not merely hearing words; it's a dedicated effort to comprehend the speaker's words, emotions, and intentions. Through active listening, you demonstrate respect and genuine interest in what the other person has to say. This practice invites open dialogue, encourages vulnerability, and lays the groundwork for authentic communication.

Key Elements of Active Listening

1. Full Presence: Dedicate your full attention to the speaker. Put aside distractions and engage with the conversation wholeheartedly.

2. Nonverbal Cues: Use nonverbal cues, such as nodding and maintaining eye contact, to signal that you are actively engaged in the conversation.

3. Clarification: Seek clarification when needed. Paraphrase what you've heard to ensure you understand the speaker's message correctly.

4. Avoid Interruptions: Allow the speaker to express themselves without interruptions. This shows respect for their perspective and encourages them to share more openly.

5. Reflect Emotions: Pay attention to the speaker's emotions and reflect them back. For instance, you might say, "It sounds like you're feeling frustrated."

The Role of Empathy

Empathy is the ability to understand and share the feelings of another person. It goes beyond intellectual comprehension and involves stepping into the other person's emotional shoes. When you practice empathy, you create a safe and supportive space where individuals feel heard, validated, and understood.

Cultivating Empathy

1. Active Imagination: Put yourself in the speaker's position and try to imagine how they might be feeling. This helps you connect on a deeper level.

2. Open-Mindedness: Be open to perspectives different from your own. This expands your understanding and allows you to appreciate diverse experiences.

3. Validation: Acknowledge the other person's emotions without judgment. Let them know that their feelings are valid, even if you don't necessarily agree.

4. Asking Questions: Ask open-ended questions that encourage the speaker to elaborate on their thoughts and emotions. This shows your genuine interest in their perspective.

Enhancing Connections Through Active Listening and Empathy

When you actively listen and practice empathy, you create an environment of trust and understanding. By showing that you care about the speaker's thoughts and emotions, you pave the way for deeper connections. These practices break down barriers, encourage vulnerability, and foster an atmosphere where individuals feel safe expressing their authentic selves.

Conclusion

Active listening and empathy are not mere communication techniques; they are profound acts of connection and understanding. By immersing yourself in the speaker's words and emotions, you demonstrate respect, compassion, and a genuine desire to connect on a deeper level. Through active listening and empathy, you enrich your relationships, forge connections that transcend surface-level interactions, and contribute to an atmosphere of authenticity and mutual respect.

7

Non-Verbal Communication

In the realm of authentic communication, words are just one part of the equation. Non-verbal communication, encompassing body language, tone, and facial expressions, plays a pivotal role in conveying authenticity. This chapter delves into the importance of non-verbal cues, highlighting how they enhance the depth and sincerity of our interactions.

The Power of Non-Verbal Cues

While spoken words carry meaning, non-verbal cues provide an additional layer of insight into our thoughts, emotions, and intentions. They serve as a rich tapestry of communication that can either reinforce or contradict our verbal messages. When aligned with our words, non-verbal cues create a harmonious and authentic interaction. However, when there's a disconnect between what we say and how we convey it non-verbally, it can lead to confusion and a lack of trust.

Body Language: Unspoken Words

Body language is a potent form of non-verbal communication. Our posture, gestures, and movements can speak volumes about our emotions and attitudes. For instance, maintaining eye contact demonstrates engagement and respect, while crossed arms might convey defensiveness. By being attuned to your own body language and recognizing others', you can enhance the authenticity of your communication.

The Impact of Tone

The way we say something can be just as important as what we say. Tone of voice conveys emotion, intent, and attitude. A friendly tone can make even a critique sound constructive, while a harsh tone can overshadow the most well-intentioned words. Being mindful of your tone and adjusting it to reflect your true feelings helps ensure that your communication is received authentically.

Facial Expressions: Windows to the Soul

Our faces are remarkably expressive, revealing emotions that words might fail to capture. Smiles, frowns, raised eyebrows – these subtle cues provide insights into our feelings. By maintaining an open and welcoming expression, you encourage others to feel comfortable sharing their thoughts and emotions authentically.

Creating Consistency

To convey authenticity effectively, it's crucial to maintain consistency between your verbal and non-verbal cues. When your words, tone, and body language align, you establish trust and credibility. However, mixed signals can erode the sincerity of your communication. Being mindful of this consistency ensures that your authentic intentions shine through.

Cultural Considerations

It's important to note that non-verbal cues can be influenced by cultural differences. Gestures, facial expressions, and even tone can be interpreted differently in various cultures. When communicating with people from diverse backgrounds, take the time to learn about their cultural norms to avoid misunderstandings.

Conclusion

Non-verbal communication is a potent tool that deepens the authenticity of our interactions. By paying attention to body language, tone, and facial expressions, we add layers of meaning to our words. These cues create an environment of openness and trust, fostering genuine connections. Remember, authenticity extends beyond what you say – it's also about how you say it. By mastering the art of non-verbal communication, you enhance your ability to forge deeper relationships and navigate conversations with true understanding.

8

Navigating Difficult Conversations

Difficult conversations are an inevitable part of life, and handling them with authenticity and sensitivity is crucial for maintaining healthy relationships. This chapter explores the art of approaching challenging topics with respect, understanding, and authenticity. By mastering strategies for staying composed, focused, and respectful during tough discussions, you can navigate these conversations with grace and effectiveness.

The Importance of Authenticity in Difficult Conversations

Approaching difficult conversations authentically sets the stage for productive dialogue. Authenticity entails expressing your thoughts, emotions, and concerns honestly, while also showing respect for the other person's perspective. This approach cultivates an atmosphere of trust and openness, even when discussing contentious issues.

Strategies for Navigating Difficult Conversations

1. Choose the Right Time and Place: Timing matters. Select a time and place

where both parties can be present and focused, minimizing distractions and interruptions.

2. Set the Tone: Begin the conversation by expressing your genuine intention to have an open and respectful discussion. This helps establish a positive atmosphere from the outset.

3. Active Listening: Listen carefully to the other person's perspective before responding. This demonstrates that you value their input and are genuinely interested in understanding their point of view.

4. Use "I" Statements: Frame your thoughts using "I" statements to express how you feel without blaming or accusing the other person. For example, say "I feel" instead of "You make me feel."

5. Stay Calm and Composed: Difficult conversations can be emotionally charged. Practice self-regulation to stay calm and composed, focusing on the issue at hand rather than getting caught up in heightened emotions.

6. Avoid Interrupting: Give the other person the space to express themselves fully. Interrupting can escalate tensions and hinder a productive discussion.

7. Acknowledge Emotions: Validate the other person's emotions, even if you disagree. Acknowledging their feelings shows that you're empathetic and open to understanding their perspective.

8. Ask Clarifying Questions: If you're unsure about a statement or perspective, ask clarifying questions to ensure you have a clear understanding before responding.

9. Stay Solution-Oriented: Focus on finding solutions and common ground. Keep the conversation forward-looking, with the goal of resolving the issue rather than assigning blame.

10. Take Breaks if Needed: If emotions run high, it's okay to take a break and regroup before continuing the conversation. This prevents escalation and allows both parties to approach the discussion with a clearer mindset.

Maintaining Respect and Empathy

Throughout difficult conversations, maintaining respect and empathy is paramount. Remember that you're discussing the issue, not attacking the person. Approach the conversation with an attitude of understanding, even if you fundamentally disagree. This respectful approach encourages reciprocal respect and opens the door for a productive exchange.

Conclusion

Difficult conversations provide an opportunity for growth, understanding, and resolution. By navigating these conversations with authenticity, sensitivity, and respect, you demonstrate your commitment to maintaining healthy relationships. Through active listening, composed demeanor, and a focus on solutions, you create an environment where challenging topics can be addressed openly and constructively. Mastering the art of navigating difficult conversations allows you to forge deeper connections, foster understanding, and cultivate an atmosphere of authenticity in all your interactions.

9

Receiving Feedback Gracefully

Receiving feedback is an integral part of authentic communication and personal growth. This chapter delves into the art of welcoming feedback with an open heart, recognizing its value in fostering self-awareness and promoting personal development. By understanding how to receive feedback gracefully, you empower yourself to navigate interactions with humility, learning, and authenticity.

The Significance of Receiving Feedback

Feedback provides a mirror to our actions and behaviors, enabling us to see ourselves from an outside perspective. While it might be uncomfortable, feedback offers insights into how others perceive us and how our actions impact them. Embracing feedback with an open heart allows us to grow, make positive changes, and strengthen our relationships.

Approaching Feedback with Authenticity

When receiving feedback, authenticity is key. An open heart and a willingness to learn create an environment where others feel comfortable sharing their observations. By embracing feedback without defensiveness, you show that you value the perspectives of those around you, even when the feedback is challenging.

Strategies for Receiving Feedback Gracefully

1. Stay Open and Listen: Approach feedback with an attitude of openness. Listen carefully to what the other person is saying without interrupting or becoming defensive.

2. Avoid Taking it Personally: Remember that feedback is about actions and behaviors, not your inherent worth as a person. Separating yourself from the feedback allows you to view it objectively.

3. Express Gratitude: Thank the person for sharing their perspective, even if the feedback is difficult to hear. Expressing gratitude shows your respect for their input.

4. Seek Clarification: If you're unclear about specific aspects of the feedback, ask clarifying questions to gain a deeper understanding.

5. Reflect Before Responding: Take some time to reflect on the feedback before responding. This prevents knee-jerk reactions and allows you to respond thoughtfully.

6. Focus on Growth: View feedback as an opportunity for personal growth and improvement. Embrace the chance to enhance your skills and relationships.

The Role of Self-Awareness

Receiving feedback gracefully is closely tied to self-awareness. Self-awareness enables you to recognize your strengths and areas for improvement. When you're aware of your own tendencies, behaviors, and triggers, you can approach feedback with a balanced perspective, separating what's constructive from what's subjective.

Promoting Personal Growth Through Feedback

Feedback is a catalyst for personal growth. By actively seeking and welcoming feedback, you expose yourself to diverse perspectives that can expand your self-awareness. This self-awareness, in turn, enables you to make intentional changes and enhance your interactions with others.

Conclusion

Receiving feedback gracefully is a skill that fosters authenticity and personal growth. By approaching feedback with an open heart, listening attentively, and focusing on self-awareness, you pave the way for self-improvement and stronger relationships. Embracing feedback as an opportunity rather than a critique allows you to nurture authenticity in your interactions and continually evolve as an individual. Through this process, you build connections rooted in understanding, respect, and a shared commitment to growth.

10

Conflict Resolution and Authenticity

Conflict is an inevitable aspect of relationships, but it is how we approach and resolve conflicts that truly defines the strength of our connections. This chapter delves into the role of authentic communication in conflict resolution, highlighting how understanding each other's perspectives contributes to effective resolution. By embracing authenticity and empathy, you can navigate conflicts with integrity and create lasting resolutions that strengthen relationships.

The Power of Authentic Communication in Conflict Resolution

Authentic communication is a linchpin in resolving conflicts constructively. When we engage in open and honest dialogue, we create a space where emotions, concerns, and perspectives can be shared without judgment. This transparency forms the foundation for productive conflict resolution, as it fosters mutual understanding and paves the way for collaborative solutions.

Promoting Resolution Through Understanding

Understanding each other's perspectives is crucial in conflict resolution.

Authentic communication allows each party to express their thoughts and feelings, providing insight into their motivations and concerns. When both parties feel heard and acknowledged, it becomes easier to identify common ground and work toward a resolution that addresses everyone's needs.

Strategies for Effective Conflict Resolution

1. Listen Actively: Engage in active listening to fully understand the other person's point of view. This demonstrates respect and lays the groundwork for a productive conversation.

2. Acknowledge Emotions: Recognize and validate each other's emotions. Acknowledging feelings creates an empathetic environment that encourages open communication.

3. Express Yourself Honestly: Communicate your thoughts and emotions authentically, while also showing respect for the other person's perspective.

4. Seek Common Ground: Identify areas of agreement or shared goals. These points of convergence can serve as a foundation for finding solutions.

5. Explore Solutions Together: Collaborate to brainstorm solutions that address both parties' concerns. A cooperative approach fosters a sense of unity and shared ownership of the resolution.

6. Focus on the Issue, Not the Person: Keep the conversation centered on the conflict at hand rather than devolving into personal attacks. This maintains a respectful atmosphere.

7. Be Willing to Compromise: Be open to finding middle ground and making concessions. Flexibility contributes to finding resolutions that satisfy both parties.

8. Avoid Blame and Defensiveness: Instead of pointing fingers, focus on how to move forward. Avoiding blame and defensiveness encourages a more solution-oriented discussion.

Strengthening Relationships Through Conflict Resolution

Authentic communication during conflict resolution has a profound impact on relationships. When conflicts are addressed with empathy, respect, and a commitment to understanding, relationships can emerge even stronger than before. Resolving conflicts authentically fosters an environment of trust and vulnerability, where both parties feel comfortable sharing their thoughts and emotions openly.

Conclusion

Conflict is a natural part of human interactions, but how we address and resolve conflicts speaks to our authenticity and character. Through authentic communication, we create the foundation for effective conflict resolution. By understanding each other's perspectives, embracing empathy, and working collaboratively toward solutions, we nurture relationships that can withstand challenges. Conflict resolution guided by authenticity not only resolves issues but also strengthens bonds, fostering connections built on mutual respect, understanding, and a shared commitment to growth.

11

Creating a Culture of Authenticity

Aculture of authenticity is one where individuals feel empowered to express themselves openly and honestly, creating an environment of trust, respect, and meaningful connections. This chapter delves into the art of cultivating such an environment within relationships, exploring practices that encourage ongoing authentic communication and foster a culture of authenticity.

The Importance of an Authentic Relationship Environment

A culture of authenticity nurtures genuine connections by prioritizing open communication and vulnerability. Such an environment creates a safe space for individuals to share their thoughts, feelings, and experiences without fear of judgment. When authenticity is celebrated, relationships flourish, and mutual understanding deepens.

Cultivating Authenticity: Shared Practices

1. Lead by Example: Demonstrate authenticity by expressing your thoughts, feelings, and vulnerabilities openly. When others see your willingness to be

genuine, they are more likely to follow suit.

2. Active Listening: Practice active listening consistently. When individuals feel heard and understood, they are more inclined to reciprocate with their own authenticity.

3. Encourage Open Dialogue: Foster an atmosphere where conversations can be candid and open. Encourage others to share their perspectives without fear of criticism.

4. Value Diversity: Embrace diverse viewpoints and encourage discussions that explore different angles. This promotes a well-rounded understanding of various experiences.

5. Embrace Vulnerability: Show that vulnerability is not a sign of weakness but rather a testament to strength and authenticity. Encourage others to share their vulnerabilities as well.

6. Respectful Communication: Set a standard for respectful communication. Address disagreements with civility and empathy, focusing on understanding rather than winning.

7. Celebrate Honesty: Celebrate honesty, even when it involves admitting mistakes. When honesty is rewarded rather than punished, it encourages ongoing authenticity.

8. Create Safe Spaces: Ensure that individuals feel safe expressing themselves without fear of ridicule or judgment. This might involve private conversations or established "ground rules" for open discussions.

Practices for Ongoing Authentic Communication

1. Regular Check-Ins: Schedule regular check-ins where individuals can

share their thoughts and feelings. This keeps communication lines open and nurtures ongoing authenticity.

2. Express Gratitude: Encourage the practice of expressing gratitude and appreciation. Gratitude fosters positive interactions and creates a foundation of respect.

3. Reflect on Communication: Encourage individuals to reflect on their communication styles and consider how they can be more authentic in their interactions.

4. Learn from Feedback: Embrace feedback and use it as an opportunity for growth. Adjust your communication based on the insights you gain.

5. Celebrate Personal Growth: Acknowledge and celebrate moments of personal growth and vulnerability. This reinforces the importance of authenticity in your relationship culture.

Conclusion

Creating a culture of authenticity requires intention, effort, and a commitment to fostering open communication. By practicing authenticity and promoting shared practices that encourage ongoing authentic communication, you cultivate an environment where individuals feel comfortable being their true selves. In such a culture, relationships thrive, trust is strengthened, and connections are deepened. By valuing authenticity and nurturing an environment of open dialogue, you pave the way for lasting, meaningful relationships built on genuine understanding and respect.

12

Reflection and Growth

As we approach the conclusion of this exploration into authentic communication within relationships, it's a fitting time to reflect on the journey we've undertaken. This chapter delves into the lessons learned and the growth experienced while integrating authentic communication into relationships. It summarizes key takeaways and provides guidance for continuing to prioritize honesty, vulnerability, and genuine connection.

Reflecting on the Authentic Communication Journey

Reflecting on the journey of integrating authentic communication into relationships, you may have discovered the transformative power of genuine expression. You might have experienced the joy of deeper connections and the resilience that comes from navigating challenges with openness. The journey has likely revealed that authenticity is not just a communication style but a way of being that shapes the fabric of your relationships.

Key Takeaways

1. Vulnerability is Strength: Embracing vulnerability allows you to forge meaningful connections that are rooted in authenticity and mutual respect.

2. Listening is a Gift: Active listening is a powerful gift you can give to others. It fosters understanding and nurtures an environment of empathy.

3. Empathy Fosters Connection: The practice of empathy creates bridges between perspectives and nurtures a culture of understanding.

4. Conflict is an Opportunity: Conflict can be a catalyst for growth when approached with authenticity and a commitment to resolution.

5. Growth Requires Reflection: Self-awareness and personal growth are nurtured through reflective practices, such as seeking feedback and learning from experiences.

Continuing the Journey of Authenticity

As you move forward, continue to prioritize honesty, openness, and connection in your relationships. Here are some guiding principles:

1. Consistency Matters: Authenticity is not a one-time endeavor; it's an ongoing commitment. Continue practicing open communication in both good times and challenging moments.

2. Embrace Imperfection: Authentic communication doesn't mean having all the answers. It's okay to admit when you don't know something or when you've made a mistake.

3. Practice Patience: Authentic relationships take time to develop. Be patient as you build trust and navigate the complexities of human interactions.

4. Value Growth Over Perfection: Focus on growth and progress rather than

striving for perfection. Allow room for mistakes and learning experiences.

5. Stay Curious: Approach your interactions with a curious mindset. Seek to understand the perspectives of others and be open to learning from their experiences.

6. Nurture Self-Care: Prioritize self-care to ensure that you're in the best emotional state to engage authentically with others.

7. Celebrate Connection: Celebrate the moments of genuine connection you experience. These connections are the fruits of your authentic communication efforts.

Conclusion

The journey of integrating authentic communication into relationships is a dynamic and fulfilling one. It's a journey that requires intention, self-awareness, and a commitment to growth. By reflecting on the lessons learned, embracing vulnerability, and continuing to prioritize open communication, you create an environment where authenticity thrives and connections flourish. As you move forward, remember that authenticity is a gift you give to yourself and others—one that fosters deep understanding, empathy, and the richness of genuine human connections.

About the Author

9 788568 957523